IMAGES
of America

THE BLAINE HOUSE

Living in the Blaine House since 2011, Gov. Paul LePage and First Lady Ann LePage have hosted many memorable events there, including a celebration of the 25th anniversary of the restoration of the mansion and a dinner observing the 150th anniversary of the Civil War. Each fall, the LePages open the house on three Saturdays to invite the public to bring donations of food for those in need. Participants are treated to a personal tour of the house by the governor. (First Lady Ann LePage.)

ON THE COVER: This postcard shows the Blaine House shortly after its 1919 renovation by the State of Maine as a home for Maine governors and their families. See page 46. (Maine Historic Preservation Commission).

IMAGES
of America

THE BLAINE HOUSE

Earle G. Shettleworth Jr.

ARCADIA
PUBLISHING

Published by Arcadia Publishing
Charleston, South Carolina

Printed in the United States of America

Library of Congress Control Number: 2013937852

For all general information, please contact Arcadia Publishing:
Telephone 843-853-2070
Fax 843-853-0044
E-mail sales@arcadiapublishing.com
For customer service and orders:
Toll-Free 1-888-313-2665

Visit us on the Internet at www.arcadiapublishing.com

This book is dedicated to Gov. Percival P. Baxter, a Blaine House resident from 1921 to 1925, through whose vision and generosity Katahdin became the mountain of the people of Maine.

CONTENTS

Acknowledgments   6

Introduction   7

1.   Mr. and Mrs. Blaine at Home   9

2.   Politician and Public Servant James G. Blaine   25

3.   Home of Maine Governors   41

4.   The Road to the Blaine House   73

5.   First Families   85

6.   First Ladies   101

7.   Famous Guests   111

8.   Blaine House Christmas Cards   117

ACKNOWLEDGMENTS

My first personal contact with a resident of the Blaine House came at an early age. Growing up in Portland, I began attending Baxter School at the age of seven in 1956. Gov. Percival P. Baxter, for whom the school was named, was an annual visitor to each classroom. Thus, I had an opportunity to meet the man who had led Maine from 1921 to 1925 and later donated Mount Katahdin and its surrounding land for Baxter State Park.

Governor Baxter's example of dedication to the state of Maine influenced me greatly in choosing a career in state government. During the past four decades, I have served under seven governors, from Kenneth Curtis to Paul LePage. During that time, I have worked with governors and first ladies regarding the history and preservation of the Blaine House. These projects have included celebrations for the 150th and 175th anniversaries of the house, the 1987 restoration committee, which became the Friends of the Blaine House, the second edition of H. Draper Hunt's *The Blaine House, Home of Maine's Governors*, and the restoration of the New England Garden. The strong public-private partnership of first families, past and present, with the Friends of the Blaine House and the Maine Bureau of General Services has assured that the Blaine House continues to fulfill its dual role as an historic treasure and a living home. Unless otherwise noted, images appear courtesy of the Maine Historic Preservation Commission.

For their help in compiling this book, I want to thank First Lady Ann LePage and her assistant Lynn Harvey. Andrew McKinnon, president of the Friends of the Blaine House, was most supportive, as were Anthony Douin of the Maine State Archives, Melanie Mohney and Anne Cough of the Maine State Library, Phyliss von Herrlich of the Kennebec Historical Society, David Richards of the Margaret Chase Smith Library, and Nicholas Noyes and Sofia Yalouris of the Maine Historical Society. Kirk Mohney and Claudette Coyne of my staff were especially helpful.

While James G. Blaine was the subject of many books during and after his lifetime, one cannot write about the Blaine House without referring to Hunt's *The Blaine House: Home of Maine's Governors*, which was first published in 1973 under the direction of First Lady Polly Curtis and was updated and reissued in 1994 under the leadership of First Lady Olympia J. Snowe. Equally valuable in telling the remarkable story of James G. Blaine's life is Neil Rolde's 2006 biography, *Continental Liar from the State of Maine*.

INTRODUCTION

The Blaine House in Augusta has long been one of the most notable residences in Maine. Since 1920, it has served as the official home of the state's chief executive, and as a symbol of government, it ranks with the statehouse. The house has been a National Historic Landmark since 1964, but, as the home of the statesman James Gillespie Blaine (1830–1893), it has been a venerated political shrine for a much longer time. Simultaneously the social showcase of Maine, a working office, and a family living quarters, the structure reflects the pride of the state in its past, present, and future.

Construction of the house began while the statehouse was being erected across the street. On August 24, 1830, Augusta merchant James Child sold a parcel of land at the corner of State and Capitol Streets to Capt. James Hall of Bath. Hall, a retired master mariner, completed building his home in 1833, a year after the statehouse was finished. In every sense, the two structures were born and brought up together. In its original form, Hall's house was a square, hipped-roof structure with a handsome colonnaded porch. At some point, Captain Hall added an ell to his retirement home.

After Hall's death, his sons conveyed the property to their mother, Frances Ann Hall. She remained there until February 22, 1850, when she sold the house to Greenwood Child, a son of the original landowner. A prosperous local merchant, Child resided there until his death in 1855. On November 20, 1862, J. Rufus Child conveyed house and land to James G. Blaine for the sum of $5,000. At that point, the building entered the mainstream of state and national history.

Congressman Blaine presented the deed to his wife, Harriet Stanwood Blaine, as a birthday present, and the family of five moved in. As the politician's family and career grew, so did the shape and size of the house. The Blaine addition, a smaller replica of the old "Hall House," was erected at the end of the ell. It featured a porch and entrance that led to the "Plumed Knight's" study and much-prized billiard room. Other changes included the addition of cupolas, the changing of porch styles, and the lowering of the chimneys. By 1872, the interior and exterior architecture bore little resemblance to Captain Hall's late-Federal-period mansion.

The Blaines also had a cottage at Bar Harbor and a mansion in Washington, DC, but the house in Augusta was always home. Here, Blaine mapped his political strategy, relaxed on the lawn, entertained, and in 1879 was the target of an aborted assassination attempt. Blaine's years of residency in Augusta were ones of tumult. When he bought the property, he had just won election to Congress after having been editor of the *Kennebec Journal* and having served in the Maine Legislature and as chairman of the Republican State Committee. He would subsequently rise to become Speaker of the House, United States Senator, Republican presidential candidate, and secretary of state under Presidents Garfield, Arthur, and Harrison.

After Blaine's death in 1893, his wife, Harriet, continued to live in the Augusta house. She died there in 1903, leaving shares of the property to several members of the family. For a time, apartments were rented to young politicians serving in the legislature. By 1917, Walker Blaine

Beale, the senator's grandson, had obtained five of the eight shares of the house. Having joined the Army, Beale offered his family home as a headquarters for the Maine Red Cross war effort. Upon his death in battle the following year, Beale's shares, as well as those of his father, went to his mother, Harriet Blaine Beale.

In 1915, the Maine Legislature required the governor to have an official residence in Augusta. The legislature had considered buying the Blaine House for such a purpose. Harriet Beale, however, chose to present the property to the State of Maine in the name of her son, Walker Blaine Beale, and as a memorial to her father. The deed was received on March 11, 1919. Contiguous property was purchased, and a neighboring building was torn down in order to improve the grounds. The noted Portland architect John Calvin Stevens was engaged to design major exterior and interior alterations. A new wing was added to the rear for service functions, the sunroom replaced the old veranda, and the house was modernized in keeping with its historic character. Over the years, subsequent administrations made interior changes, particularly in the work and living areas. The exterior was little altered since the family of Gov. Carl Milliken first resided there in 1920. During the administration of Gov. John R. McKernan Jr., a major effort was started in 1988 to return the interior to its 1919 appearance. More recently, First Lady Karen Baldacci restored the 1920 New England Garden designed for Governor Milliken by the Olmsted Brothers. Today, Gov. Paul LePage and First Lady Ann LePage work in cooperation with the Friends of the Blaine House and the Maine Bureau of General Services to preserve and enhance the Blaine House and its grounds as a state treasure for the people of Maine.

One

MR. AND MRS. BLAINE AT HOME

Maine became a state in 1820; seven years later, Augusta was chosen as its capital. Between 1829 and 1832, the Maine State House, shown in this 1836 painting by Charles Codman, was constructed at the corner of State and Capitol Streets. Immediately to the right of the statehouse is the two-story, hip-roofed, late-Federal-style home built in 1833 by Capt. James Hall, a retired sea captain. The house remained in the Hall family until 1850, when the captain's widow, Frances, sold it to Greenwood Child, an Augusta merchant.

On November 20, 1862, Greenwood Child's son J. Rufus Child sold Captain Hall's "Mansion House" at State and Capitol Streets to James G. Blaine for $5,000. That day, Blaine deeded the property to his wife, Harriet, as a birthday present. Taken from the statehouse roof, this pre-1864 photograph shows the home in the foreground as it was when acquired by the Blaines—a two-story main house with a two-story ell and a two-bay carriage house.

Taken from atop the statehouse, this 1871 photograph of the Blaine House by Skowhegan photographer S.S. Vose reflects the changes made to the house in 1869. That year, the Blaines added a one-story Victorian porch to the ell and remodeled the carriage house from a gable roof to a hip roof.

A second remodeling of the Blaine House took place in 1872, as seen in this picture by Augusta photographer Henry Bailey. That year, the Blaines added an Italianate bay window and cupola to the main house and a two-story addition to the ell, which contained a first-floor study and billiard room and a second-floor bedroom suite. This addition featured a cupola, which echoed the one on the main house.

During the 1872 remodeling, the carriage house at the left was detached from the ell and moved west on the property to make way for the two-story addition, as shown in this photograph by F.A. Morrill of New Sharon. The carriage house was enlarged by a third in size during the same renovation.

11

This panoramic view of Augusta from the statehouse in 1880 includes the Blaine House in the lower left. In 1884, Thomas W. Knox wrote of the city in a biography of James G. Blaine: "Augusta is the spot about which his strongest home associations cluster. This attractive little city of some ten thousand inhabitants is charmingly located on both banks of the Kennebec. Its streets are wide, the private residences substantial, there is an abundance of old elms and maples."

The Blaines' closest neighbors were Joseph A. Homan and his family, who lived in the house at the right, built in the 1830s by James L. Child. The Homan House was acquired by the State of Maine in 1919 and removed to provide privacy for future governors and their families as well as to create land for the New England Garden.

As the influential publisher of the *Maine Farmer*, a popular Augusta weekly newspaper, James A. Homan shared James G. Blaine's enthusiasm for public affairs and the press. Here, Homan stands in the front parlor of his State Street home with his wife, Susan Sewall Homan, at the left, and two of her relatives, Caroline Sewall Manley and Abigail Manley.

The Capitol Street side of the Blaine House is shown in this late-19th-century photograph, which documents the appearance of the Blaine House from 1872 to 1919. Blaine biographer Thomas Knox writes, "In 1872 Mr. Blaine contemplated the removal of the old, and building of a new house, but on reflection concluded to enlarge it by building a rear portion to give more room, making the whole harmonious in exterior, and convenient within."

This 1887 photograph of the Blaine House from Capitol Street shows the carriage house at the left, which was converted into a garage when the State of Maine acquired the property in 1919. Blaine biographer E.K. Cressey remarked in 1884 that "Mr. Blaine is careful about his exercise and takes walks and rides. He has a large barn for horses and generally keeps a number of them."

News of James G. Blaine's nomination for president reached Augusta from Chicago on Friday afternoon, June 5, 1884. Biographer Russell H. Conwell describes the scene: "When the important dispatch was handed him, he was resting in a hammock . . . on the lawn before his door. He talked coolly and cheerfully about that and other matters with the neighbors who freely came into his yard to congratulate him."

The celebration of James G. Blaine's nomination for president reached a climax on June 21, 1884, with the visit of the convention's notification committee, consisting of a delegate from each state. Standing on the lawn outside his house, Blaine accepted the nomination from chairman John B. Henderson of Missouri. His son, Walker Blaine, stood behind him holding a letter of acceptance.

In June 1884, the eyes of the nation were focused on Augusta, Maine. During the days that followed Blaine's choice as the Republican nominee for president, large crowds of well-wishers came to the house to support their candidate. As shown in this engraving from the June 21, 1884, issue of Frank Leslie's *Illustrated Newspaper*, Blaine addressed his followers from the front steps of his home.

While secretary of state under President Garfield, James G. Blaine built this imposing brick Victorian mansion in 1881 on Washington's fashionable DuPont Circle from designs by architect John Fraser. The house still stands today, the last of the grand DuPont Circle homes. The Blaines soon found this house too large for their needs and rented it to a Chicago millionaire while living in a leased townhouse on Lafayette Square near the White House.

When James G. Blaine became secretary of state under Pres. Benjamin Harrison in 1889, he leased 17 Madison Place, a historic 1831 townhouse on Lafayette Square, close to the White House and the Department of State. Its most famous occupant was Secretary of State William H. Seward, who hosted Pres. Abraham Lincoln there frequently during the Civil War. Blaine died in the Madison Place house on January 27, 1893.

As Bar Harbor emerged in the 1880s as one of America's leading resorts, James and Harriet Blaine built this summer home there. Named for Harriet Blaine's family, Stanwood was constructed in 1885–1886 from designs by William Camac of the Philadelphia architectural firm of Furness, Evans and Company. Seen here from the ocean side, this grand Queen Anne cottage was destroyed in the 1947 Bar Harbor fire.

Stanwood's gabled roofline was equally picturesque from the land side. According to biographer Henry Davenport Northrop, "Mr. Blaine was very fond of Bar Harbor. His cottage is chiefly remarkable for its great veranda. During the summer Mr. Blaine lived on his porch a great deal of the time." Stanwood remained in the Blaine family after James and Harriet Blaine's deaths, the last owners being the Blaines' daughter Margaret and her husband, Walter Damrosch.

As secretary of state, James G. Blaine entertained Pres. Benjamin Harrison at his Bar Harbor cottage for six days in August 1889. In this image, the presidential party is assembled on Stanwood's stone porch overlooking the ocean. Shown, from left to right, are President Harrison; Harriett Stanwood Blaine; James G. Blaine; Anna Davis Lodge and her husband, Henry Cabot Lodge; the president's private secretary, E.W. Halford; Margaret Blaine; Walker Blaine; and James G. Blaine Jr.

The *New York Times* reported on August 18, 1889, that President Harrison had spent his Bar Harbor vacation attending luncheons and dinner parties hosted by the wealthy summer community. Here, the presidential party pauses for a photograph in front of Stanwood. Pictured, from left to right, are (front row) James G. Blaine Jr., Anna Davis Lodge, President Harrison, Harriet Stanwood Blaine, James G. Blaine, and Harriet Blaine; (back row) Henry Cabot Lodge, Walker Blaine, and the president's private secretary, E.W. Halford.

In his 1893 biography of James G. Blaine, Henry D. Northrop describes Blaine and his family in Augusta: "He entered into the life of the little city as heartily as did any of the inhabitants. Mr. Blaine was often on the street, and he seldom rode. Mrs. Blaine mingled freely among many friends, while the sons and daughters did not hold themselves off from the other youth of the city."

Harriet Stanwood Blaine was born in Augusta in 1827 as the daughter of a wool merchant. As a young woman, she taught in Millersburgh, Kentucky, where she met James G. Blaine. Three years after their marriage in 1851, the Blaines moved to Augusta, where he became the editor of the *Kennebec Journal* before entering politics in 1858. Throughout her husband's public career, Harriet was known for her sage advice and generous hospitality. She outlived him by a decade, dying at the Blaine House in 1903.

James and Harriet Blaine had seven children, the first of whom, Stanwood, died at three. Their second child, Walker Blaine, was born in Augusta in 1855, graduated from Yale, and attended Columbia Law School. When his father served as secretary of state in the Garfield, Arthur, and Harrison administrations, Walker was the elder Blaine's most trusted assistant and confidant. At his death in 1890, Walker was a highly respected lawyer and diplomat.

The Blaine's third child, Emmons Blaine, was born in Augusta in 1857, educated at Harvard and Harvard Law school, and pursued a career as a corporate executive for several railroads in Chicago. In 1886, Emmons married Anita McCormick of Chicago, the daughter of Cyrus McCormick, the inventor of the reaper and a man of great wealth. Their marriage ended with Emmons's death in 1892.

The fifth Blaine child was Margaret, born in Augusta in 1865. She is depicted here receiving the news of her father's presidential nomination in 1884. At Bar Harbor in 1889, Margaret Blaine met Walter Damrosch, a noted German American composer and the longtime conductor of the New York Philharmonic Orchestra; they were married in Washington in 1890. The Damrosches summered in Bar Harbor their entire married life, with Margaret dying in 1949 and Walter the following year.

Born in Prussia in 1862, Walter Damrosch came to New York with his musical family in 1871 and became conductor of the Metropolitan Opera in 1885. From 1902 to 1928, he served as the conductor of the New York Philharmonic Orchestra. His compositions included five dramatic operas, and he achieved national fame with his pioneer radio broadcasts, which fostered music appreciation between 1926 and 1942.

Named for this father, James G. Blaine Jr. was born in Augusta in 1868 as the sixth child of James and Harriet Blaine. Young "Jamie" Blaine shocked his family in 1886 when at the age of 18 he married Marie Nevins in New York after meeting her in Augusta only 18 days before. The marriage ended in divorce in 1892. Jamie later moved to California, where he died in 1926.

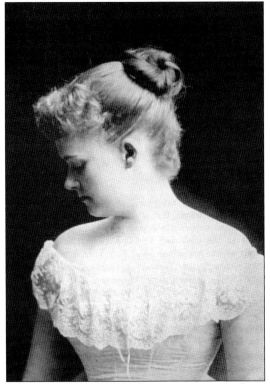

At age 19, New York actress Marie Nevins created a sensation by marrying the 18-year-old son of James G. Blaine, one of the nation's most well-known politicians. The marriage soon failed— with Jamie Blaine returning to his parents and Marie conducting a press campaign against the Blaine family—and ended in divorce in 1892. Marie fared better in her second marriage to the noted New York surgeon Dr. William T. Bull, which lasted until her death in 1911.

The youngest of the Blaine children was Harriet, who was born in Augusta in 1871 and died in New York in 1958. Her marriage to Washington diplomat Truxtun Beale in 1894 ended in divorce in 1896. Their son, Walker Blaine Beale, became the owner of the Blaine House. After his death in battle in France in 1918, Harriet Blaine Beale inherited the house and gave it to the State of Maine in 1919 as the residence for Maine governors and their families.

James G. Blaine is seated on the porch of his Bar Harbor cottage in 1892, the last summer of his life. At this point, Blaine was a household name in American politics, both revered and reviled. His more than three decades in public life included representing Maine in the United States House from 1863 to 1876, and in the Senate from 1876 to 1881. After unsuccessful tries for the Republican presidential nomination in 1876 and 1880, Blaine lost the presidency to Grover Cleveland in 1884. Historians give Blaine high marks for his accomplishments as secretary of state in the Garfield, Arthur, and Harrison administrations.

Two

POLITICIAN AND
PUBLIC SERVANT
JAMES G. BLAINE

In post–Civil War America, the mark of celebrity was to have a cigar named for oneself. This decorative cigar box label, dating from about 1890, declares James G. Blaine to be "The Greatest Statesman of Them All." The books at the left symbolize the two aspects of Blaine's public life. *Twenty Years in Congress*, published in two volumes in 1884 and 1886, represents his political career, while *Pan-American Congress* refers to one of his major diplomatic achievements as secretary of state under Pres. Benjamin Harrison.

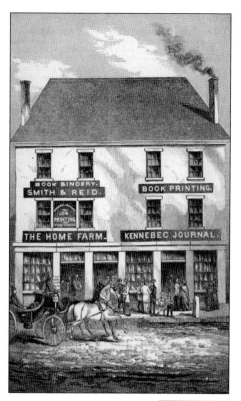

On November 10, 1854, the *Kennebec Journal* announced that the newspaper had been sold to Joseph Baker and James G. Blaine. A newcomer to Augusta, Blaine was described as talented, educated, well traveled, and acquainted with the leaders and issues of the day. The young newspaper editor worked in this building on Water Street from 1854 to 1857, establishing himself as an essential player in the new Republican Party in Maine.

James G. Blaine's brief career as editor of the *Kennebec Journal* and the *Portland Advertiser* laid the foundation for his entrance into politics at the age of 28 in 1858, when this picture was taken. That year, he was elected to the Maine House of Representatives as a Republican and served there from 1859 to 1862. Blaine also became chairman of the Republican State Committee in 1859, a post he held until 1881.

This earliest photograph of the Maine State House in Augusta, taken during the Civil War, shows the building as it looked when James G. Blaine served there in the Maine House of Representatives. Constructed of Hallowell granite between 1829 and 1832, the statehouse was designed by Boston architect Charles Bulfinch. Only the portico and front wall survive today due to remodeling in 1890 and 1909.

James G. Blaine's rapid rise in politics is reflected in his election as speaker of the Maine House of Representatives in 1861 and 1862. In Blaine's time, the House chamber was located on the second floor of the statehouse, directly below the dome. The speaker presided from an elevated desk in front of a heavily draped window, and the public observed proceedings from columned visitors galleries on the sidewalls.

When James G. Blaine arrived in Washington in 1863 to begin his first term in the US Congress, he was no stranger to Pres. Abraham Lincoln. Blaine became a Lincoln supporter in 1858 after witnessing a Lincoln-Douglas debate in Illinois. Two years later, Blaine was a member of the Republican committee that notified Lincoln of his nomination for president. When President Lincoln needed a manager for his 1864 reelection campaign in Maine, he chose Blaine.

Ulysses S. Grant's success as commander of the Union army during the Civil War earned him two terms as president between 1869 and 1877. The start of Grant's first term coincided with James G. Blaine's election as Speaker of the House in 1869, a post he held until 1875, when the Democrats gained control of the House.

While James G. Blaine considered his three terms as Speaker of the House the happiest period of his life, powerful political forces were splitting the Republican party into two factions: the Stalwarts, who supported President Grant, and the Half-Breeds, who questioned the president's policies. Blaine sided with the latter camp, resigning from the House in 1876 to replace Lot M. Morrill in the Senate.

In 1876, James G. Blaine actively campaigned for the Republican nomination for president. Affectionately called "the Plumed Knight" by his supporters, Blaine was the leading contender for the nomination when the party convention opened in Cincinnati. However, allegations of financial misconduct marred his chances, and former Ohio governor Rutherford B. Hayes secured the nomination on the seventh ballot and went on to win the presidency in the fall.

While serving in the US Senate from 1876 to 1881, James G. Blaine remained one of the nation's leading political figures. In the *Dictionary of American Biography*, Carl Ross Fisher describes Blaine as seen in this 1879 illustration, calling him "a commanding figure" and writing that "his eyes were particularly brilliant; his voice effective and attractive. His manner had much of the dignity of his generation of statesmen. Much more striking, however, was his magnetic quality, which made his oratory perhaps the most thrilling of the day."

The 1880 Republican presidential nomination produced a highly competitive race between James G. Blaine, former president Grant, and Sen. John Sherman. On the 34th ballot, James A. Garfield's name was unexpectedly put forward, and Blaine threw his support to his friend Garfield, who won the nomination on the 36th ballot. Once elected president, Garfield appointed Blaine as his secretary of state.

On March 5, 1881, James G. Blaine resigned his Senate seat to become President Garfield's secretary of state. Seen here at 50 years old in 1881, Blaine confidently looks squarely into the camera of noted portrait photographer Napoleon Sarony. As secretary of state, Blaine embarked on a strong foreign policy in which America's goals were to control any Central American canal and to expand its influence and trade in the hemisphere.

On July 2, 1881, James G. Blaine accompanied President Garfield to the Washington railroad station to see the president off on a trip north. With Blaine at his side, Garfield was shot by Charles J. Guiteau, a disgruntled office-seeker who favored the Stalwart politics of Vice Pres. Chester A. Arthur. Garfield lived for 11 weeks, dying on September 19, 1881.

Vice Pres. Chester A. Arthur became president upon James A. Garfield's death on September 19, 1881. Because Arthur favored the Stalwart wing of the Republican Party, James G. Blaine recognized that he had no influence in the new administration and offered his resignation on September 22, 1881. At the president's request, Blaine remained as secretary of state until December 19, 1881.

James G. Blaine stands at the Speaker's rostrum of the House of Representatives on February 27, 1882, to deliver the memorial address for Pres. James A. Garfield. Blaine's choice as the orator for this national occasion reflects his friendship with the Garfield family and his eloquence as a speaker. Of the fallen president, Blaine said, "No foreboding of evil haunted him; no slightest premonition of danger clouded his sky. His terrible fate was upon him in an instant."

The presidential nomination that had eluded James G. Blaine in 1876 and 1880 became his in 1884. When many Republicans decided that year that their sitting president, Chester A. Arthur, was a weak candidate, the party nominated Blaine on the fourth ballot at their Chicago convention. So confident of a victory were Blaine's supporters that they issued this portrait of their nominee captioned "Our Next President" and paired it with one for their vice presidential candidate, John A. Logan.

James G. Blaine's vice presidential running mate was John A. Logan of Illinois, whose public career included election to the US House and Senate and duty as a Civil War general. In May 1868, Logan initiated the observance of Memorial Day. General Logan was an ideal vice presidential candidate, having congressional experience that paralleled Blaine's, military service where Blaine had none, and a Midwestern state to complement Maine.

ALBANY

Presidential campaigns in the 19th century were usually low-key events, with nominees greeting supporters on their front porches. However, James G. Blaine recognized that he faced a formidable Democratic opponent in Gov. Grover Cleveland of New York. Here, Blaine takes the fight to Cleveland's home territory of Albany as part of a strenuous seven-week campaign tour by train through the Northeast and the Midwest.

Thomas Nast, America's leading political cartoonist of the post–Civil War period, unleashed opposition from *Harper's Weekly* against James G. Blaine in a series of satirical campaign cartoons. Here, on June 28, 1881, a grumpy Blaine rests his arm on two thick volumes of his questionable public record and defiantly asks, "Well, what are you going to do about it?"

The presidential campaign of 1884 was one of the dirtiest in American history. Dubbed "Continental Liar from the State of Maine," Blaine was plagued by lack of support from reform Republicans, called "Mugwumps," and charges of financial corruption, anti-Catholicism, and influence from wealthy donors. Blaine supporters retaliated with the claim that Grover Cleveland had fathered a child out of wedlock, giving rise to the slogan, "Where's My Pa?"

When election day November 4, 1881, was over, James G. Blaine had narrowly lost to Grover Cleveland. Democratic victory hinged on the 1,149 votes by which Cleveland won New York, assuring him of an electoral count of 219 over Blaine's 182. Thomas Nast had the last word in his *Harper's Weekly* cartoon of November 8, 1884, which asks, "Are 20 Years of Blaine Enough?" referring to Blaine's memoir *Twenty Years in Congress*.

Throughout most of James G. Blaine's 35 years in public life, his closest political confidante was Joseph H. Manley of Augusta. A successful businessman, postmaster, state legislator, and leader in the Maine and national Republican parties, Manley is described in the 1897 publication *Men of Progress* as "a warm friend and intimate of James G. Blaine, from whom he learned the art of politics."

37

Roscoe Conkling of Utica, New York, and James G. Blaine entered the US House of Representatives together in 1863. A growing rivalry between them flared in 1866 in a series of heated public exchanges on the House floor, which resulted in Conkling's refusal to ever speak to Blaine again. Elected to the Senate in 1867, Conkling became Blaine's chief political enemy for the next two decades.

During the last decade of his life, one of James G. Blaine's closest friends was Andrew Carnegie, the famed Scottish American industrialist and philanthropist. Carnegie supported Blaine for president in 1884, believing that his compatriot from Maine was gifted with an intellectual brilliancy that set him apart from other American politicians of the time. When Blaine lost the presidency, Carnegie invited him for a long stay at his Scottish estates.

In 1888, James G. Blaine declined to seek the Republican nomination in favor of Benjamin Harrison of Indiana, a Civil War general and former senator. Blaine actively campaigned for Harrison's election. When Harrison won, he appointed Blaine as secretary of state. Given Blaine's extensive experience in public life, critics asserted that he would dominate both President Harrison and his cabinet, which created tensions between the two leaders.

James G. Blaine's second term as secretary of state lasted from March 7, 1889 to June 4, 1892. Shown here at work in his office, Blaine pursued a foreign policy that sought an American controlled canal in Central America and an American presence in the Caribbean and the Pacific. Blaine chaired the first Pan-American Conference in Washington in 1889. Such accomplishments were the capstones of his long public career.

Taken by Napoleon Sarony, one of the last photographs of James G. Blaine shows a man weary beyond his 62 years. Blaine suffered a series of illnesses during his second term as secretary of state, which was between 1889 and 1892. His chronic ill health, coupled with the tragic loss of three of his children—Walker and Alice in 1890 and Emmons in 1892—led to his death on January 27, 1893.

Three

HOME OF
MAINE GOVERNORS

Shortly after taking office in 1987, Gov. John R. McKernan Jr. stands next to the portrait of James G. Blaine, which hangs over the State Dining Room fireplace. The following year, Governor McKernan established the Blaine House Restoration Fund. This private, nonprofit corporation was charged with planning the restoration of the house and grounds, raising funds to finance the effort, and developing an endowment to provide for the long-term care of the property. In 1993, the Friends of the Blaine House was created to ensure that this work would continue.

After James G. Blaine's death, his widow rented the Blaine House to John F. and Laura L. Hill from 1897 to 1902. Hill was elected governor in 1900, and the Hills used the house as their official residence until they moved to their new home on State Street in January 1903. That summer, Harriet Stanwood Blaine returned to the Blaine House and died there on July 15, 1903.

Harriet Stanwood Blaine willed the house in 1903 to her three children and two of her grandsons. For the next 15 years, the Blaine family made the house available for various purposes, including renting it for three months in 1905 to six young legislators and providing the study as an office for Gov. Bert M. Fernald during the statehouse remodeling in 1909 and 1910.

Walker Blaine Beale was born in the Blaine House on March 22, 1896, the son of Truxtun and Harriet Blaine Beale. For his 21st birthday in 1917, the young man received the controlling interest in his grandparents' home. That year, he made the house available to the State of Maine for use as offices in the war effort. On September 18, 1918, Beale was killed while fighting in the St. Mihiel Drive in France.

On March 11, 1919, Gov. Carl E. Milliken received a letter from Harriet Blaine Beale offering the Blaine House to the State of Maine as a governor's residence in memory of her son. The Maine legislature enthusiastically accepted the gift, and Governor Milliken set about the task of converting the house and grounds into a suitable home for his and future gubernatorial families.

When the State of Maine acquired the Blaine House, no changes had been made to the exterior since the 1872 remodeling. Taken in 1919 by the Stevens architectural firm, this photograph shows the State Street facade of the house, Captain Hall's 1833, late-Federal-style residence with the added Italianate features of a bay window at the left and a cupola on the roof.

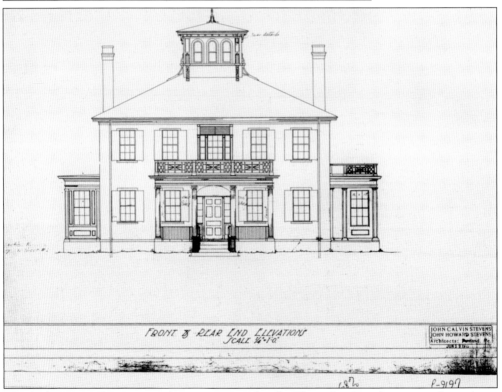

FRONT & REAR END ELEVATIONS
SCALE ¼"·1'·0'

JOHN CALVIN STEVENS
JOHN HOWARD STEVENS
Architects: Portland, Me.
JUN 19 19

P-9197

The dual purpose of preserving a historic memorial to the Blaine family and creating a functioning governor's mansion guided John Calvin Stevens in his 1919 renovation of the Blaine House. This June 19, 1919, drawing reflects the architect's desire to recapture the Federal-style character of the original home by introducing an open porch and remodeling the left bay window while retaining the Italianate cupola.

Another 1919 photograph of the Blaine House taken by the Stevens architectural office shows the 1872 addition with its elaborate Italianate portico, arched window, and cupola. Stevens would install an Ionic portico and remove the window, but retain the cupola. To the right is the porch, which would be replaced by the classical colonnade and French doors of the sunroom.

AUGUSTA, ME. EX. GOVERNOR HILL'S RESIDENCE.

When Gov. John F. and First Lady Laura L. Hill built this grand mansion at State and Green Streets in Augusta between 1901 and 1902, their intention was that it would be offered to the State of Maine for a governor's residence upon their deaths. This plan was precluded in 1919 when the state acquired the Blaine House for that purpose. John Calvin Stevens designed this $250,000 home.

In *The Maine Book* of 1920, state librarian Henry E. Dunnack describes the remodeled Blaine House: "When standing at the corner of State and Capitol Streets the visitor notices two things first of all, the raising of the middle section of the building to the height of the front and rear portions, and the changing of the color from the old battleship gray to a colonial white."

This 1920s view of the south side of the Blaine House was taken from the statehouse across Capitol Street. Henry Dunnack notes that at the left "a wing has been added to the northwest corner of the house for the accommodation of the servants, laundry and other necessary rooms for carrying on the work and care of the structure."

Governor Milliken commissioned the Olmsted Brothers, a noted landscape architecture firm, to plan the Blaine House grounds. The Olmsteds' New England Garden appears on the north side of the house in this 1930s photograph, taken from State Street. As Henry Dunnack writes, "From the outside the house has the appearance of an old colonial mansion, pure white with green blinds and shaded by the great trees in the neighborhood."

John Calvin Stevens of Portland was considered Maine's leading architect when he was retained by the state in 1919 to remodel the Blaine House. In a distinguished career that spanned from 1880 to 1940, Stevens designed all manner of buildings, but his specialty was domestic architecture. After 1900, much of his residential work was in the popular Colonial Revival style.

Few photographs survive of the interior of the Blaine House prior to the 1919 remodeling. This rare view of the entrance hall was taken that year by the Stevens architectural firm. Victorian features include the hat stand and the cast-iron radiator at the left, the hanging gas fixture, the wicker chair under the staircase, and the figured wallpaper.

In the remodeled entrance hall, the original winding staircase remains in place, as does the bust of Lord Byron over the doorway and the statue of Minerva in the niche on the stairs. The figured wallpaper has been replaced with plain painted walls, and the large bronze plaque in memory of Walker Blaine Beale is in place on the wall at the left.

While John Calvin Stevens designed the 1919 architectural changes to the Blaine House, the furnishing and decoration was placed in the charge of the Boston interior decorating firm of Pennell, Gibbs, & Quiring. The Blaines transformed the front and back parlors into the large space that became the State Reception Room, shown in this 1920 photograph furnished with oriental rugs, Colonial Revival furniture, and elegant drapes. The columns date from the Blaine period.

On the north side of the house, the Blaines merged a front sitting room and a dining room into one large dining room, which became the State Dining Room, shown here in 1920. Pairs of columns like those in the State Reception Room were removed by John Calvin Stevens, and the architect reproduced the Federal-style woodwork of the former sitting room throughout the dining room.

In his 1919 remodeling of the Blaine House, John Calvin Stevens redesigned the connector between the original house and the Blaines' 1872 addition. On the first floor, this resulted in the sunroom with its tiled floor, stone fireplace mantel, and beamed ceiling. At the left, sunlight streams into the room through a glass wall of three pairs of sash doors and two stationary doors.

On the first floor of the north side of the connector, John Calvin Stevens created the family dining room for daily use by the first family and for their smaller-scale entertaining. The room was lighted by a projecting bay of five large windows that overlook the New England Garden. While most interiors in the 1919 remodeling were painted, the family dining room featured wallpaper.

On the second floor, the new connector provided private quarters for the first family, including this attractive family living room. On April 21, 1921, the *Kennebec Journal* reported, "Neutral tone paper is on the walls of the Governor's living room. The hangings are of gold. There is a huge Davenport in front of the fireplace, and back of the Davenport is a table of the Adam design."

The front section of the Blaine House contained four second-floor bedrooms, the front two of which became guest rooms in the 1919 remodeling. The southeast guest room, shown here, was known as the Blue Room. On March 10, 1937, the *Kennebec Journal* commented, "These guest chambers have given rest and relaxation to visiting notables who once were housed in local hotels or private homes."

This 1983 photograph of the Blaine House shows the front of the house as it appeared from 1919 to 1989. In 1964, Secretary of the Interior Stewart Udall designated the Blaine House a National Historic Landmark. According to the January 29, 1964, *Kennebec Journal*, Udall declared that "the Blaine House has been found of exceptional value in commemorating and illustrating the history of the United States."

The south side of the Blaine House, seen here in 1983, has remained unchanged from 1919 to the present, a pleasing combination of Federal, Victorian, and Colonial Revival features. In 1927, Frederick L. Collins wrote of the house: "Only in Maine and Texas, where the Blaine and Houston mansions have a historic as well as an architectural beauty, have I found official residences worthy of these great states."

Over time, the original decorating scheme of Pennell, Gibbs, & Quiring underwent changes. By 1983, the restrained hallway décor of 1919 had given way to a long oriental carpet, an oriental runner on the staircase, and a reproduction of 19th-century yellow wallpaper featuring a classical motif. The Victorian chair at the left is one of a pair of hall chairs owned by the Blaines.

Historic features blend with more recent ones in this 1983 photograph of the State Reception Room. The pairs of black marble fireplaces and circular plaster ceiling ornaments are original to the house, while the Corinthian columns were added when the Blaines merged the front and back parlors into one large room. The glass chandeliers date from the mid-20th century.

By 1983, the State Dining Room had assumed a comfortable elegance with its custom-made Priscilla Turner carpet, cheerful flowered wallpaper, and glass chandelier. Since 1922, the Battleship Maine silver at the right has been displayed in this room. Ordinarily, a state presented a silver punch bowl and cups to its namesake vessel, but prohibitionist Maine chose a soup tureen and two vegetable dishes instead.

Located on the first floor of the 1872 addition, the Blaine study retained its Victorian appearance in the 1919 remodeling in response to the wishes of James G. Blaine's daughter, Harriet Blaine Beale, the donor of the house. In 1940, Beale and her sister, Margaret Blaine Damrosch, paid to refurbish the room, signing a statement that reads, "The Victorian wallpaper is a reproduction from a room in Washington once occupied by Abraham Lincoln, and other furnishings are in accord with the decorative spirit of the period."

In 1920, Carl Rust Parker, the landscape architect in charge of the Blaine House grounds for the Olmsted Brothers, designed a new front entry on State Street with granite steps, Colonial Revival balustrades, and arbors. In 1989 and 1990, the Blaine House Restoration Fund's grounds committee oversaw the construction of Parker's transforming design by the Cianbro Corporation of Pittsfield.

Governor McKernan wrote in 1994, "Because the Blaine House is so steeped in history, and because of the special feeling that Maine citizens have towards it, we began an effort to restore and freshen both the interior and the gardens of this historically significant public building." A photograph taken that year shows the refurbished entrance hall with its elegant white wallpaper highlighted with gold medallions.

Between 1989 and 1993, the Blaine House Restoration Fund accomplished the most significant work on the house since its acquisition by the state. Nowhere was this more apparent than in the State Reception Room, where the moss green walls and the ivory woodwork replicated the 1919 colors uncovered by paint analysis. A recent gift of two oriental rugs has brought this room even closer to its 1919 appearance.

The green and silver color scheme in the State Dining Room was chosen to represent the trees and lakes of Maine. The striped wallpaper was manufactured in 1908 and found in a warehouse in Cincinnati. This historic paper was hung on the dining room walls 82 years later in 1990. The woven vine border is a reproduction of a historic paper.

As seen in this 1994 photograph, the restoration brought back the 1919 colors of the sunroom walls and ceiling, providing an attractive setting for a Colonial Revival–furnishing scheme and the three hanging electrical fixtures of the period. Made for the State Dining Room, the 1960 Priscilla Turner rug was moved to the sunroom and has been replaced by an heirloom oriental carpet.

In 1989, the family dining room was redecorated with print drapes and wallpaper featuring a traditional rope and tassel pattern. That year, at Governor McKernan's suggestion, the center window was converted into a doorway to provide direct access to the New England Garden.

One of the treasures of the Blaine House is displayed on James G. Blaine's senate desk at the right in his study—a pass written by Pres. Abraham Lincoln on April 7, 1865, to authorize Congressman Blaine to visit the recently captured Confederate capital of Richmond, Virginia. Lincoln was assassinated a week later. The print over the fireplace depicts Lincoln reading the Emancipation Proclamation to his cabinet.

Adjacent to the Blaine Study is the game room, which was restored to its Victorian appearance in 1979 and 1980 by Gov. Joseph E. Brennan, who was an avid pool player. The restoration uncovered the original 1872 two-toned mahogany and birch floor and matching wainscoting, which had been obscured by carpeting and tile. James G. Blaine called this room his gymnasium.

For nearly a century, loyal staff members have been crucial to running the Blaine House. When Gov. Sumner Sewall and First Lady Helen E. Sewall began residence there in 1941, they brought their housekeeper, Maude Longley, with them. When she arrived at the Blaine House, Maude had already worked 41 years for the Sewall family. Her years in Augusta were made memorable by hosting such guests as Eleanor Roosevelt, Harry Truman, and Fiorello La Guardia.

Veteran Blaine House cook Margery Tucker displays a plate of her baked potatoes to First Lady Jane Muskie in 1958. Margery served six first families—from the Paynes to the Curtises. Muskie commented that the teas, card parties, luncheons, and charitable fund raising events made the Blaine House like "the grand ballroom of a big city hotel except that it has a built-in hostess." (Maine State Museum.)

Phyllis H. Siebert served as the Blaine House chef for five first families from 1972 to 2001. Here, she prepares a meal in the Blaine House kitchen for Governor Brennan in 1983. In 1997, Phyllis published *Recipes and Reminiscences, A Blaine House Cook Book*, which is a valuable record of 25 years of Blaine House history as well as a source of many wonderful Maine recipes. (Kennebec Historical Society.)

The Blaine House has been open to the public since 1920 and is a favorite destination of school groups and tourists who visit Augusta. In this 1986 photograph, Blaine House staff member Mary Piselli gives children from a summer recreation program a tour of the Blaine Study. (Kennebec Historical Society.)

The Blaine House has been the scene of many cultural events celebrating Maine's support for the arts. Here, Gov. Joseph E. Brennan, left, and members of his cabinet listen to a performance of the Portland String Quartet in the State Reception Room in 1984. The concert was part of a series sponsored by the governor and the Maine Arts Commission. (Kennebec Historical Society.)

Four

THE ROAD TO
THE BLAINE HOUSE

Since the Blaine House became Maine's official gubernatorial residence in 1919, twenty governors have been elected to office. Here, Lewis O. Barrows gives a campaign speech in his 1936 election bid. That year, Barrows won the Blaine House for the Republican Party, and Maine was one of only two states in the nation that went for Alf Landon, the Republican candidate for president.

A native of Pittsfield, Carl E. Milliken (1877–1961) graduated from Bates College and worked in the lumber business in Aroostook County. He served in the Maine House and Senate before running for governor on the Republican ticket in 1916. That year, he unseated incumbent Democratic governor Oakley C. Curtis. Two years later, Milliken won reelection by defeating Democrat Bertram G. McIntire. Milliken is remembered for his dynamic leadership of Maine during World War I.

Frederick H. Parkhurst (1864–1921) was born in Unity, educated in Bangor, and received his law degree from George Washington University in 1887. He practiced law in Bangor and served in the Maine House and Senate. A Republican, Parkhurst won the 1920 campaign for governor against Democrat Bertram G. McIntire, but died after less than a month in office in January 1921.

Courting new women voters was not lost on Gov. Percival P. Baxter (1876–1969), shown here with YWCA ladies during the 1922 campaign. A Portland attorney, Baxter was serving as Senate president in 1921 when he became governor upon Frederick Parkhurst's death. Republican Baxter won a term in his own right in 1922 by defeating Democrat William R. Pattangall. Baxter later gave the land for the state park in northern Maine that bears his name.

Ralph Owen Brewster (1888–1961), left, passes a leaflet to a voter in his 1924 quest for the governorship. A Dexter native, Brewster attended Bowdoin College and Harvard Law School before establishing his law practice in Portland in 1913. After serving in the Maine House and Senate, he was elected governor on the Republican ticket in 1924, defeating Democrat William R. Pattangall. Brewster won a second term in 1926 against Democrat Ernest L. McLean.

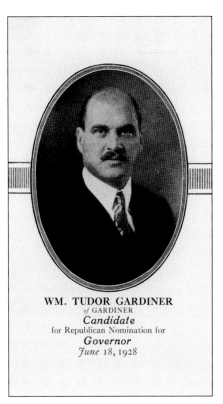

WM. TUDOR GARDINER
of GARDINER
Candidate
for Republican Nomination for
Governor
June 18, 1928

William Tudor Gardiner (1892–1953) is pictured on a brochure promoting his candidacy for the Republican nomination for governor in 1928. A member of a distinguished Maine family, Gardiner attended Harvard and Harvard Law School. After serving as an Army officer in World War I, he entered the Maine House. Gardiner was elected governor in 1928 and was reelected in 1930, his opponent in both races being Democrat Edward C. Moran.

OUR GOVERNOR

LOUIS J. BRANN
LEWISTON, MAINE

Louis J. Brann (1876–1948) was born in Madison, educated in Gardiner, and attended the University of Maine. He began practicing law in Lewiston in 1902, using the city as a political base for his election to several local and state offices. In 1932, Democrat Brann defeated Republican Burleigh Martin for the governorship and won a second term in 1934 against Republican Alfred K. Ames.

Lewis O. Barrows
Republican Candidate
For Governor

Six years a Member of the
Republican State Committee

Six years a Member of the
Governor's Council

Elected Secretary of State by the
Eighty-Seventh Legislature

Your Support will be Appreciated

Born in Newport, Lewis O. Barrows (1893–1967) attended Hebron Academy and the University of Maine before joining his family pharmaceutical business. As reflected in this campaign postcard, Barrows served on the executive council and as secretary of state before running for governor as a Republican in 1936. That year, he defeated Democrat F. Harold Dubord and Independent Benjamin C. Bubar. Governor Barrows was reelected in 1938 in a contest with former governor Louis Brann.

Sumner Sewall (1897–1965) came from a noted shipbuilding family in Bath, Maine. Educated at Yale, Sewall was a pilot in World War I and later became an airline executive. His service in the Maine House and Senate in the 1930s led to his election as governor on the Republican ticket in 1940. That year, his Democratic opponent was Fulton J. Redmond. This 1942 postcard was used in Sewall's reelection campaign, in which he defeated Democrat George W. Lane Jr.

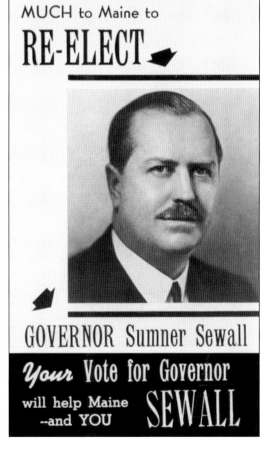

TODAY it Matters
MUCH to Maine to

RE-ELECT ➤

GOVERNOR Sumner Sewall

Your Vote for Governor
will help Maine
--and YOU SEWALL

Horace A. Hildreth (1902–1988) spent his childhood in Gardiner and attended Bowdoin College and Harvard Law School. He practiced law and served in both houses of the Maine Legislature before running for governor as a Republican in 1944. That year, he used this postcard in his successful campaign to defeat Democrat Paul J. Jullien. In 1946, Hildreth won a second term in a decisive victory over Democrat F. Davis Clark.

A Lewiston native, Frederick G. Payne (1904–1978) attended the Bentley School in Boston, which prepared him to become financial manager for a chain of New England movie theaters. He served three terms as mayor of Augusta and was an Air Force officer during World War II. A Republican, Payne used this postcard to promote his successful bid for the governorship in 1948 against Democrat Louis B. Lausier. Payne won a second term in his 1950 contest with Democrat Earle S. Grant.

VOTE REPUBLICAN

☒

Your Vote will keep Maine on the National Team

Experience Counts

RE-ELECT **BURTON M. CROSS** RE-ELECT
GOVERNOR OF MAINE

Born in Gardiner, Burton M. Cross (1902–1998) graduated from Cony High School in Augusta and became a florist in 1926. Active in community service, he served on the Augusta City Council and in the Maine House and Senate. In a three-way race in 1952, Republican Cross won the governorship against Democrat James G. Oliver and Independent Neil Bishop. This 1954 postcard dates from Cross's unsuccessful bid for reelection.

Edmund S. Muskie (1914–1996) attended Rumford schools and graduated from Bates College and Cornell Law School. After serving as a naval officer in World War II, he returned to Waterville to practice law and enter politics. Experience in the Maine House led to his 1954 election as the Democratic candidate for governor, defeating incumbent Burton M. Cross. Muskie repeated his victory in 1956 by defeating Republican William A. Trafton for a second term. (Maine State Archives.)

Clinton A. Clauson (1895–1959) was raised on an Iowa farm and served in World War I. In 1919, he moved to Waterville, where he conducted a chiropractic practice. A term as mayor of Waterville in 1956–1957 led to his nomination as the Democratic candidate for governor in 1958. That year, he won election against former governor Horace A. Hildreth, a Republican. Clauson died on December 30, 1959, just short of a year in office. (Maine State Archives.)

As Senate president, John H. Reed (1921–2012) succeeded Clinton Clauson as governor. A native of Fort Fairfield, Reed graduated from the University of Maine and saw naval duty in World War II. After the war, he joined his family's potato business and entered Republican politics, serving in the Maine House and Senate. Reed was elected in 1960 to finish Clauson's term in a race against Democrat Frank M. Coffin. In 1962, Reed defeated Democrat Maynard C. Dolloff for a four-year term.

KEEP MAINE MOVING!
Re-Elect
GOVERNOR JOHN H. REED

LEADERSHIP – ENERGY – ABILITY

Kenneth M.

CURTIS
for
GOVERNOR

Democrat Kenneth M. Curtis unseated incumbent governor John H. Reed in 1966 and was reelected in 1970 in a race against Republican James S. Erwin. A native of Leeds, Curtis attended Maine Maritime Academy, served as a naval officer in the Korean War, and graduated from Portland University Law School. An attorney, Curtis became secretary of state in 1965 and governor in 1967.

LONGLEY
FOR GOVERNOR
THiNK ABOUT IT!

Longley for Governor Committee
P. O. Box 1975   Lewiston, Maine 04240

James B. Longley (1924–1980) grew up in Lewiston and served in the Army Air Corps during World War II. After the war, he attended Bowdoin College and established a successful insurance business in Lewiston. In 1972, Governor Curtis appointed Longley to chair the Maine Management and Cost Survey. Longley used this cost reduction panel experience to launch his independent bid to win the 1974 gubernatorial election against Democrat George J. Mitchell and Republican James S. Erwin.

Born in Portland's Munjoy Hill neighborhood, Joseph E. Brennan attended Boston College and the University of Maine Law School. Service in the Maine House and Senate and as attorney general laid the groundwork for his election as the Democratic nominee for governor in 1978. His opponents that year were Republican Linwood E. Palmer and Independent Herman C. Frankland. Democrat Brennan won a second term in 1982 in his race against Republican Charles L. Craigin.

Born in Bangor, John R. McKernan Jr. attended Dartmouth College and the University of Maine Law School. After two terms in the Maine House and two terms in the US House, he was elected governor in 1986 as a Republican in a four-way race against Democrat James Tierney and Independents Sherry Huber and John Menario. McKernan won a second term in 1990 in a challenge from former Democratic governor Joseph E. Brennan and Independent Andrew Adam.

A Virginia native, Angus S. King Jr. graduated from Dartmouth College and the University of Virginia Law School. King was an attorney, businessman, and popular television host before winning the governorship as an independent in 1994 by defeating former Democratic governor Joseph E. Brennan, Republican Susan M. Collins, and Green Independent Jonathan K. Carter. King was reelected in 1998 in a four-way race against Republican James B. Longley Jr., Democrat Thomas J. Connolly, and Green Independent Patricia H. LaMarche.

John Elias Baldacci grew up in Bangor, attended the University of Maine, and managed his family's restaurant. He entered public service at 23, serving on the Bangor City Council, in the Maine Senate, and in the US Congress prior to his election as governor in 2002. That year, Baldacci was the victor in a four-way race with Republican Peter Cianchette, Green Independent Jonathan K. Carter, and Independent John Michael. The governor won reelection in 2006 over four opponents—Republican Chandler Woodcock, Independent Barbara Merrill, Green Independent Pat LaMarche, and Independent Philip Morris Napier.

83

Born in Lewiston, Paul R. LePage overcame a childhood of poverty and domestic violence to earn a bachelor of science degree in business administration from Husson College and an MBA from the University of Maine. His successful career as a business consultant and manager led to his becoming general manager of the popular chain of Marden's stores in 1996. LePage entered public life with his election to the Waterville City Council in 1998, followed by three terms as Waterville's mayor. He won the governorship in 2010 as a Republican in a five-way race with Independent Eliot Cutler, Democrat Elizabeth Mitchell, Independent Shawn Moody, and Independent Kevin Scott.

Five

FIRST FAMILIES

The Millikens were the first family to live in the Blaine House after it became the governors' residence in 1919. They moved in early in January 1920, just in time for the birth of their seventh child, Dorothy Blaine Milliken, on January 22. This photograph, taken in the sunroom in 1920, shows, from left to right, Gladys E. Milliken, Vivian C. Milliken, Nelly K. Milliken, Charles E. Milliken Jr., First Lady Emma C. Milliken holding Dorothy, Edith L. Milliken, Gov. Carl E. Milliken, and Beatrice E. Milliken.

Pictured, from left to right, are Frederick H. Parkhurst, Edith W. Parkhurst, and Dorothy Woodman Parkhurst. Taken in the Parkhursts' garden on West Broadway in Bangor, this photograph shows the family prior to the birth of a second daughter, Patricia, in 1919. Governor Parkhurst died after less than a month in office on January 29, 1921.

Gov. Percival P. Baxter's Blaine House companions were his dogs. He is seen here with Sandy, who accompanied him to the Republican National Convention in Cleveland, Ohio, in July 1924. The governor holds a campaign portrait of Calvin Coolidge, the Republican presidential nominee that year.

This photograph of the Brewster family at the front entrance to the Blaine House appears on their Christmas card from 1927. Pictured, from left to right, are First Lady Dorothy F. Brewster, Owen Brewster, Gov. Ralph Owen Brewster, and Charles F. Brewster.

In 1928, the Gardiner family sits for this formal studio portrait, which is featured in a campaign brochure for William Tudor Gardiner's successful bid for the governorship that year. Pictured, from left to right, are Margaret Thomas Gardiner holding Sylvester Gardiner, Tudor Gardiner, Margaret Gardiner, Thomas Gardiner, and future governor Gardiner.

Gov. Louis J. Brann reads a newspaper while First Lady Martha Cobb Brann sews in this 1935 photograph, taken in the Blaine House Reception Room. Absent from the picture are the Branns' three daughters—Marjorie, Dorothy, and Nancy.

Gov. Lewis O. Barrows and First Lady Pauline Pomeroy Barrows are seated in the Blaine House Reception Room in 1937 with their three sons—from left to right, Wallace H., Robert W., and Edward P. A student at Williams College, Robert died that year in an automobile accident; Edward was killed in action in 1944 while fighting in France during World War II.

Gov. Sumner Sewall and First Lady Helen Evans Sewall are shown in the Blaine House sunroom with their children—from left to right, David, Nicholas, and Alexandra. The picture was taken between 1941 and 1945.

The Hildreth family are gathered for this 1946 campaign photograph. Pictured, from left to right, are Josephine, First Lady Katharine Wing Hildreth, Gov. Horace A. Hildreth, Anne, Katherine, and Horace A. Jr.

Gov. Frederick G. Payne and First Lady Ella Hodgdon Payne share a light moment together in this 1951 photograph by Clarence F. McKay Sr. Absent from the picture is son E. Thomas Payne.

Gov. Burton M. Cross and First Lady Olena Moulton Cross are shown in the living room of the Blaine House family quarters with, from left to right, son-in-law Richard Butler and daughters Barbara Cross Butler, Nancy, and Burtina. This photograph was taken for the Crosses' 1953 Christmas card by Clarence F. McKay Sr.

A 1958 photograph of the Muskies on the front porch of the Blaine House captures the exuberance of this attractive young family. Gov. Edmund S. Muskie and First Lady Jane Gray Muskie are shown with their children, from left to right, Ellen, Stephen, and Melinda. This picture was taken before the birth of their fourth child, Martha, later in 1958.

Gov. Clinton A. Clauson and First Lady Ellen Kelleher Clauson enjoy Thanksgiving dinner with family members in the Blaine House State Dining Room in November 1959. Governor Clauson died on December 30, 1959, near the end of his first year in office.

Gov. John H. Reed and First Lady Cora Davison Reed are joined by their daughters Cheryl, left, and Ruth Ann for this photograph in the Blaine House Reception Room. The Reed family lived in the Blaine House from 1960 to 1967.

The Blaine House Reception Room is the setting for this photograph of Gov. Kenneth M. Curtis and First Lady Pauline Brown Curtis, with their daughters Susan, left, and Angel. Susan died in 1970. (Maine State Museum.)

Gov. James B. Longley and First Lady Helen Walsh Longley are shown in the Blaine House Reception Room in 1975 with their children, from left to right (front row) James B. Jr., and Steven; (second row) Nancy, Kathryn, and Susan.

Gov. Joseph E. Brennan enjoys a happy moment in 1980 with his daughter, Tara, and his son, Joe, at the Blaine House piano.

Gov. John R. McKernan Jr., Sen. Olympia Snowe, and Peter McKernan enjoy a family barbecue by the steps outside the Blaine House Family Dining Room in 1990. While a student at Dartmouth College, Peter died of a heart attack in 1991.

The energetic spirit of the King family is captured in this informal photograph taken in 1995 of Gov. Angus S. King Jr. and First Lady Mary Herman with their children, from left to right, James, Molly, Angus S. III, Benjamin, and Duncan.

Gov. John Elias Baldacci and First Lady Karen Weston Baldacci are shown in the Blaine House Reception Room in 2007 with their son, Jack, and English springer spaniels Sam and Mia.

The Blaine House Reception Room is the setting for this 2011 portrait of the LePage family. Pictured, from left to right, are (front row) daughters Lindsay and Lisa, grandson Nicholas Harvey, First Lady Ann LePage, granddaughter Olivia Harvey, the first lady's mother, Rita DeRosby, and son Devon Raymond; (back row) son-in-law Brian McCluskey (married to Lindsay), son-in-law Brandon Harvey (married to Lisa), Gov. Paul LePage, daughter Lauren, and son Paul II. The LePages' dog, Baxter, sits in the foreground.

Six

FIRST LADIES

One of the many duties of Maine's first ladies is to hold Blaine House teas to benefit worthy causes across the state. Here, First Lady Pauline Barrows stands at the center of a group of women who are attending such a tea in the State Dining Room in 1937. During the Barrows administration, guests at afternoon teas often were entertained by chamber music played by girls from the Oak Grove School in Vassalboro. On March 16, 1940, Alice Frost Lord wrote in the *Lewiston Journal*, "In the Blaine House as hostess, Mrs. Barrows received warm appreciation of her hospitality and her kindness." (Maine State Museum.)

Emma Chase Milliken (1876–1930) sits with her husband, Gov. Carl E. Milliken, and six of their seven children. A native of Lewiston, Emma was the daughter of George Chase, the president of Bates College. She graduated from Bates in 1897 in the same class as her husband and taught school before their marriage in 1901.

First Lady Dorothy Foss Brewster (1889–1971), right, is among prominent Maine residents calling on Pres. Calvin Coolidge, center, at the White House in 1926. Her husband, Gov. Ralph Owen Brewster, stands second from the left. Born in Portland, Dorothy graduated from Wellesley College in 1911. After her marriage in 1915, she became active in civic, political, and fraternal organizations and was noted for her gardens at the Brewsters' home in Dexter.

Margaret Thomas Gardiner (1889–1981) came from a Maine seafaring background. When she was 15, her family launched a schooner that bore her name. Before World War I, Margaret traveled extensively with her parents, collecting rare oriental porcelain. Upon her marriage to William Tudor Gardiner in 1916, she joined one of the state's prominent families. As first lady, she was admired as "sincere, broad minded, a gracious, dignified hostess, with a genuine appealing personality."

Martha Cobb Brann (1882–1961) was born in Auburn and educated in local schools. At 20, she married a young Lewiston attorney, Louis Brann, who was starting his career as a trial lawyer. Martha devoted herself to raising their three daughters while her husband pursued his legal and political careers. Sen. Margaret Chase Smith remembered Martha as "a charming and wonderful hostess, always meticulously groomed and equally concerned with the appearance of the Blaine House." (Maine State Library.)

Pauline Pomeroy Barrows (1893–1987) relaxes for a photograph in the sunroom of the Blaine House during a social event in 1937. During her four years as first lady, Pauline entertained extensively at the Blaine House and took pleasure in accompanying her husband throughout the state on his official duties. Tragedy struck in 1937 when their son Robert, a college freshman, was killed in an automobile accident. (Maine State Museum.)

Helen Evans Sewall (1897–1976) was born in Poland, the daughter of a prominent Polish diplomatic and military family. In 1929, she married Sumner Sewall, who returned to Bath in 1933 after an aviation career to enter politics. The Sewalls' four years in the Blaine House coincided with World War II, and Helen was active in supporting the war effort, commenting, "It's the greatest privilege and the greatest obligation to be an American."

First Lady Helen Sewall's commitment to America's winning World War II extended to her helping to bring in the harvest on Maine farms. Here, Sewall is picking string beans in 1943 with members of the Women's Emergency Farm Service of the Women's Land Army. Alexandra, the Sewalls' 13-year-old daughter, joined her mother in the fields. The Sewalls also grew a victory garden at the Blaine House.

Katherine Wing Hildreth (1904–1989) is shown with her husband, Gov. Horace A. Hildreth, and is about to fly to the 1946 National Governors Conference in Miami. A 1925 Vassar College graduate, Katherine was married in 1934. After four years as Maine's first lady, she presided at Bucknell University and the US embassy in Pakistan as her husband moved from governor to university president to ambassador. (Maine Historical Society.)

Ella Hodgdon Payne (1908–2004) displays the Battleship Maine silver in this 1951 photograph, taken in the State Dining Room of the Blaine House. Ella came to Waldoboro from Aroostook County in 1932 to open a beauty shop. She married Frederick G. Payne in 1944, and they moved into the Blaine House five years later. Ella felt at ease there, doing housework, cooking, gardening, knitting, needlepoint, and listening to Red Sox games on the radio.

Olena Moulton Cross (1907–1998) is joined by her husband, Gov. Burton M. Cross, in the private quarters of the Blaine House. Born in New Hampshire, Olena graduated from Cony High School in Augusta in 1926 and married the next year. She worked in partnership with her husband to manage their floral business and was active in many organizations. As first lady, Cross built a model Civil Defense air-raid shelter in the Blaine House basement, the nation's first in a governor's residence. (Maine State Museum.)

When Jane Gray Muskie (1927–2004) graduated from Waterville High School in 1945, she worked at Alvina and Delia's, the city's leading dress shop. There, she met Edmund S. Muskie, a young lawyer returned from World War II and entering politics. Within six years of their marriage in 1948, Jane Muskie became the nation's youngest first lady at 27 years old. Here, she stocks canned goods with her children, Stephen and Ellen, in the basement air-raid shelter at the Blaine House.

A native of Haverill, Massachusetts, Cora Davison Reed (1920–2004) was working at the Newport Supply Depot in Rhode Island when she met Ens. John H. Reed of Fort Fairfield. Married in 1944, the Reeds settled after World War II in Fort Fairfield, where the future governor joined his family's potato business and entered politics. During her seven years as first lady, Cora oversaw a major redecoration of the Blaine House and the construction of a Japanese garden on the grounds. (Maine State Museum.)

Known as "Polly," Pauline Brown Curtis grew up in Kennebunk and married naval veteran and law student Kenneth M. Curtis in 1957. Ten years later, the Curtises and their two daughters started life in the Blaine House. During her eight years as first lady, Polly became interested in compiling a history of the house, which was accomplished in 1973 with the publication of *The Blaine House, Home of Maine's Governors* by H. Draper Hunt.

Helen Walsh Longley (1922–2005) was raised in Ohio and met her future husband, James B. Longley, in 1943 at Wright-Patterson Airfield, where he was training as an airman. Six years later, they were married and settled in Auburn, Maine, with James launching his highly successful insurance career. In 1974, he ran successfully as an independent candidate for governor. As first lady, Helen was especially supportive of Special Olympics.

An Augusta native, Olympia J. Snowe was Maine's Second District congresswoman when she married Gov. John R. McKernan on February 24, 1989. They are shown here in the sunroom of the Blaine House in 1994 with the Battleship Maine silver in the foreground. During her five and a half years as first lady, Snowe gracefully balanced her congressional and state duties, giving strong support to her husband's restoration of the Blaine House and overseeing the publication of an updated edition of H. Draper Hunt's history of the house.

Four first ladies are photographed together during the 2008 celebration of the 175th anniversary of the Blaine House. They are, from left to right, Karen Baldacci, Mary Herman, Connie LaPointe, and Olympia Snowe. A native of Milwaukee, Wisconsin, Herman came to Maine in 1970. In 1982, she joined Cohen-Herman Associates, an Augusta-based lobbying firm. Two years later, she married Angus S. King Jr., who was elected governor in 1994. During her eight years as first lady, Herman devoted her time to raising two young children and advocating for small businesses, local artisans, the arts, literacy, and women's and children's issues.

Karen Weston Baldacci speaks at a ceremony to celebrate the restoration of Pemaquid Point Lighthouse in Bristol. Born in Kittery and raised in Dexter, she met her husband, John E. Baldacci, while attending the University of Maine at Orono, and they were married in 1983. As she holds degrees in nutrition and teaching, Karen championed the causes of childhood education, literacy, nutrition, and locally grown foods as first lady from 2003 to 2011. Working with the Friends of the Blaine House, she enhanced the grounds by building a greenhouse and restoring the New England Garden.

A native of Vassalboro, Ann LePage has served as Maine's first lady since 2011. She has been a passionate advocate for military service members, their families, and veterans. She has participated in the Wreaths Across America trip, which provides Maine-made wreaths to decorate graves at Arlington National Cemetery. LePage also encourages childhood literacy by frequently reading to children in schools and at the Blaine House.

Seven

FAMOUS GUESTS

Between 1897 and 1902, Gov. John F. Hill rented the Blaine House from Harriet Stanwood Blaine. On August 26, 1902, Pres. Theodore Roosevelt arrived in Augusta to spend the night with the Hills. Here, the president straightens his tall silk hat as he leaves the front door the next morning. The door is held open by Frederick Brown, the Blaines' longtime butler and coachman. Roosevelt told the crowd, "For my good fortune I knew Mr. Blaine quite well when he was secretary of state."

Theodore Roosevelt's stop at the Blaine House on August 26, 1902, was part of a New England speaking tour, which included appearances in Portland earlier that day and speeches in Waterville, Bangor, and Ellsworth the following day. Here, the president stands at the back of his railroad car waving his hat to the crowd as the train pulls out of the Augusta station on the morning of August 27, 1902.

Shortly after the Civil War ended, Union commander Ulysses S. Grant visited Augusta for the first time in August 1865. On his third trip to the city in the summer of 1873, then president Grant was hosted by Speaker of the House James G. Blaine. Grant stayed with the Blaines from August 12 to August 15, 1873, occupying the bedroom suite in the newly constructed addition to the house.

Another Union Civil War hero, Gen. William T. Sherman, stayed with the Blaines for a night during the summer of 1867. The *Kennebec Journal* for July 8, 1867, reports that in the evening "Mr. Blaine announced that the doors of his residence were open and invited all to step in and be personally presented to the General."

113

Seated at the center in this photograph taken on the Blaine House lawn adjacent to Capitol Street is Vice Pres. Calvin Coolidge, soon to become president of the United States. Hat in hand, Gov. Percival P. Baxter stands center right as the host of a luncheon for Coolidge and other New England governors on July 2, 1923. This was Coolidge's second visit to the house, having been there as a guest of Governor Milliken in 1920. Other presidential visitors include Ulysses S. Grant in 1873, Herbert Hoover during the Barrows administration, Harry Truman and Eleanor Roosevelt in 1942, and John F. Kennedy in 1959.

The sunroom of the Blaine House was the scene of a press conference by Sen. John F. Kennedy on November 15, 1959. A contender for the 1960 Democratic presidential nomination, Kennedy appeared with Gov. Clinton Clauson, Sen. Edmund Muskie, and Congressman Frank Coffin before addressing a Maine Democratic Party dinner at the Calumet Club in Augusta that evening. Here, Kennedy campaigns for president in Portland in September 1960.

Sen. Margaret Chase Smith was no stranger to the Blaine House, having visited Gov. Louis Brann and First Lady Martha Cobb Brann there as early as 1934. Here, Smith celebrates her 96th birthday in the State Reception Room on December 14, 1993, with Gov. John R. McKernan. She was the first woman to serve in both the House and the Senate, having been in the former from 1940 to 1949 and in the latter from 1949 to 1973. (Margaret Chase Smith Library.)

Eight

BLAINE HOUSE CHRISTMAS CARDS

The tradition of Blaine House Christmas cards began in 1923, four years before Pres. Calvin Coolidge issued the first White House holiday greeting in 1927. Maine's first official Christmas card is a postcard of Gov. Percival P. Baxter seated with his Irish setter, Garry. Originally published for Maine school children, the card was adapted for Christmas use by overprinting the message "Christmas Greetings from Governor Baxter."

Christmas Greetings

From Governor Baxter

GOVERNOR PERCIVAL P. BAXTER AND HIS IRISH SETTER "GARRY."

Governor Baxter's Message to the School Children of Maine
"Who learns and learns
Yet does not what he knows,
Is one who plows and plows
Yet never sows."
FROM THE PERSIAN.

Gov. Ralph Owen Brewster and First Lady Dorothy Foss Brewster produced four Christmas cards during their stay in the Blaine House between 1925 and 1929. Their 1926 card features a decorative cartouche containing their holiday greeting, below which appears the Maine State Seal. The card includes a painting of Mount Katahdin, labeled as "the sunrise peak of America."

Of the four Christmas cards sent by Gov. William Tudor Gardiner and First Lady Margaret Thomas Gardiner between 1929 and 1933, this one best reflects the elegance and grace that the Gardiners brought to the Blaine House. A simple "Christmas Greetings" from the governor and first lady is engraved below an embossed blue and gold state seal.

EXECUTIVE MANSION

Greetings.

The four Christmas cards issued by Gov.Louis J. Brann and First Lady Martha Cobb Brann between 1933 and 1937 employ views of the Maine State House and the Blaine House to symbolize the governorship. This 1934 card from the Branns shows the Blaine House with the statehouse in the background at the left. The Maine State Seal and "Greetings" are embossed in gold.

GOVERNOR and MRS. LEWIS O. BARROWS EXTEND BEST WISHES FOR THE NEW YEAR

The first of Gov. Lewis O. Barrows and First Lady Pauline Pomeroy Barrows' Christmas cards is illustrated with this 1937 scene of the Blaine House in winter, seen from the Capitol Street side. The statehouse dome casts a lengthened shadow on the snow-covered lawn in the foreground. This charming image is also on cards used by Gov. John McKernan and Sen. Olympia Snowe in 1989, and by Gov. John and Karen Baldacci in 2003.

Gov. Sumner Sewall and First Lady Helen Evans Sewall's years in the Blaine House, 1941–1945, coincided with World War II. In 1943, the Sewalls used this powerful patriotic image on their Christmas card, with the American and Maine flags shown against the clouds of war that have gathered over the wintry coast of Maine. The message inside is a simple one: "May Peace and Gladness enter your home this coming year."

Between 1945 and 1949, Gov. Horace Hildreth and First Lady Katherine Hildreth's four Christmas cards conveyed the family aspects of the holiday season. In 1948, the Hildreths sought to personalize their greeting by reproducing the signature of each family member, including those of their four children— Dodie, Hoddie, Anne, and Dassey.

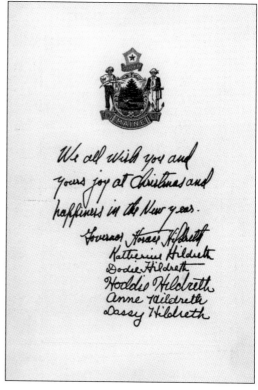

During their four years in the Blaine House, 1949–1953, Gov. Frederick G. Payne and First Lady Ella Hodgdon Payne created Christmas cards that featured charming sketches of the Blaine House, the statehouse, and the state of Maine. This 1949 card shows a map of the state flanked on either side by pen-and-ink sketches of the governor and the first lady.

With Sincere Good Wishes for a Merry Christmas and a Happy New Year

Governor and Mrs. Frederick G. Payne

Season's Greetings
FROM
GOVERNOR AND MRS. BURTON M. CROSS AND FAMILY

For their two Christmas cards, Gov. Burton M. Cross and First Lady Olena Moulton Cross chose the traditional approach of a family group photograph taken in the Blaine House. While their 1953 card shows the family in the living room of the private quarters, this 1954 picture finds the Crosses assembled in front of one of the fireplaces in the State Reception Room. (Maine State Museum.)

Gov. Edmund S. Muskie, First Lady Jane Gray Muskie, and their growing family spent Christmases between 1955 and 1958 in the Blaine House. Of their four Christmas cards, this one from 1957 best captures both the dignity and the energy that characterized the Muskies. A gold state seal is encircled by a red wreath of festive green holly.

Gov. Clinton A. Clauson and First Lady Ellen Kelleher Clauson had only one Christmas in the Blaine House due to his death on December 30, 1959. Their 1959 Christmas card shows the welcoming front porch of the Blaine House with a wreath on the door and columns decorated with evergreens. Inside, the card conveys a heartfelt message of "joyful hours, happy memories, thoughts of old friends, and a contented heart."

BLAINE HOUSE

The seven Christmas cards sent by Gov. John H. Reed and First Lady Cora Davison Reed between 1960 and 1966 feature a picture of the Blaine House on the cover and a group picture of the governor, the first lady, and their daughters, Cheryl and Ruth Ann, on the inside. Reminiscent of the Paynes' 1952 card, this pen-and-ink drawing of the house was chosen by the Reeds for their 1960 "season's greetings" to the state.

A silver state seal and a red "greetings" comprise the design for the 1972 card from Gov. Kenneth M. Curtis and First Lady Polly Curtis. The eight cards sent by the Curtises between 1967 and 1975 use a range of familiar motifs, including the statehouse, the Blaine House, the state seal, and the family photograph.

Winter in Maine is the theme of this Christmas card used by Gov. James B. Longley and First Lady Helen Walsh Longley between 1975 and 1979. Two horses pull a sleigh of winter travelers through the heavy snow of an evergreen forest in a scene reminiscent of a 19th-century Currier & Ives print.

Joe and Tara Brennan's growing-up can be traced through the eight Christmas cards sent by Gov. Joseph E. Brennan between 1979 and 1986. This 1980 photograph, taken in the living room of the family quarters of the Blaine House, is typical of the family pictures found on the cards sent by Governor Brennan.

Several of Gov. John R. McKernan and Sen. Olympia J. Snowe's eight Christmas cards between 1987 and 1995 are illustrated with paintings by Maine artists. Here, *Winter Dories, Bass Harbor* by Wini Smart of Northeast Harbor graces the cover of McKernan and Snowe's 1993 card.

Between 1995 and 2003, Gov. Angus S. King Jr. and First Lady Mary Herman continued the practice of using a work of art by a current Maine artist on their Christmas cards. Each year, King and Herman selected a different contemporary interpretation of the Blaine House. This pen-and-ink drawing of the house by Falmouth Foreside artist Shirley Leighton appears on their 1995 card.

Hallowell artist Paul Plumer's *Blaine House in Spring* was commissioned by Gov. John Elias Baldacci and First Lady Karen Weston Baldacci for their 2005 Christmas card and reflects Karen's enthusiasm for landscape gardening. In 2008, this watercolor painting was made into a commemorative print for the 175th anniversary of the house. Several of the Baldaccis' cards between 2003 and 2011 make use of works by contemporary Maine artists.

Gov. Paul R. and First Lady Ann LePage's choice for their 2012 Christmas card was the painting *The Christmas Box* by Maine artist Kay Morris. The LePages coupled this nostalgic watercolor with the following inspiring message: "May the freedom that makes our country great fill your heart and home with the hope and promise this holiday season and always."

DISCOVER THOUSANDS OF LOCAL HISTORY BOOKS
FEATURING MILLIONS OF VINTAGE IMAGES

Arcadia Publishing, the leading local history publisher in the United States, is committed to making history accessible and meaningful through publishing books that celebrate and preserve the heritage of America's people and places.

Find more books like this at
www.arcadiapublishing.com

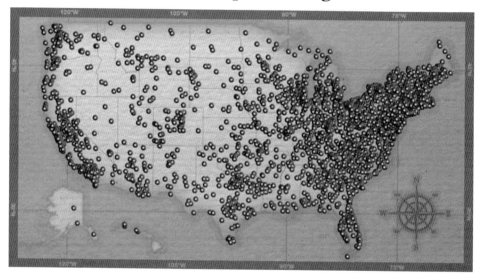

Search for your hometown history, your old stomping grounds, and even your favorite sports team.

Consistent with our mission to preserve history on a local level, this book was printed in South Carolina on American-made paper and manufactured entirely in the United States. Products carrying the accredited Forest Stewardship Council (FSC) label are printed on 100 percent FSC-certified paper.

MADE IN THE

USA